Step N2 UR Destiny

Breaking every chain

Cherlene Adewunmi

Step N2 UR Destiny
By Cherlene Adewunmi

Distributed by 2sides2theCross and CAE Publications

Printed in the United States of America

ISBN: 0988612909

ISBN 13: 9780988612907

Cover Design – Cherlene Adewunmi

Unless otherwise indicated, all Scripture quotations are taken from the Life Application Study Bible, NLT, copyright © 2004, GNT, NLV, NIV, World English Bible, New American Standard Bible, and Ampli ied Bible copyright 1987.

Acknowledgments

I take this opportunity to give thanks to my heavenly Father, the great I AM. Thank You, Lord and Savior Jesus Christ, for without Your shedding of blood I would not be alive. The more I die to self, the more You become alive in me. Holy Spirit, thank You for being my comforter, my enabler, and my everyday power. God, You are awesome!

A special thanks to my husband, priest, friend, and life partner, Sola Adewunmi. You have taught me a lot, and for this I am for-ever thankful.

To my eight wonderful children, I love you and thank God for your lives. I pray that my life has and will continue to be a reflection of the true love of God. I pray that you not only accept Jesus Christ as your Savior, but that you also accept His Lordship. For when He is your Lord, all will go well with you. May you impact your generation with the power that comes from within.

Content

Preface

This book was written to encourage everyone—young, old, men, and women alike. I pray that you take to heart all the information provided here and apply it to your life.

It is very important to understand that children are influenced first and foremost by their home environment, or lack thereof. Most children grow up and become what they are accustomed to seeing.

In this book are some keys to help you step into your God-ordained destiny, as these were the keys that unleashed me into mine.

For the principles in this book to work, *you* must decide that you will be the one to take action. It is not about placing blame on those you believe are responsible for your life; it is about *you* no longer being the victim and breaking the chains of bondage off your life. It is about destroying the powers of darkness over your life and the lives of the generations that will come after you.

Preface

Father, in the name of Jesus, I pray for those who have dared to read this book, that their hearts, minds, and eyes will be opened to a new truth, a new way of living, and a new destiny. Touch each and every one of them, and as that touch brings about change, may the change remain for generations to come. Amen.

Chapter One
Identify and Acknowledge

Generational curses are the expressions of misfortune due to a willingness to sin that fall on a person or group of people. They are generational in nature because they latch onto a lineage and travel for years, decades, and even centuries.

Generational curses have the ability to skip a generation and are countless in number.

These curses are hidden under anger, suicide, teenage pregnancy, neglect, abuse, addictions, mental illness, perversion, pride, poverty, hereditary diseases, arrogance, homosexuality, and such.

No area of our life is off-limits, and if we truly want total freedom, we must be willing to embrace the truth about generational curses, face the demons, and plead the blood of Jesus. Then and only then will we be able to step out of darkness and embrace a brighter tomorrow.

The truths about generational curses are avoided like a plague; they are often covered up, and sometimes we pretend they do not exist at all. Consequently, many lives are out of control and destroyed because of them.

Parents who are drug addicts often raise children who become drug addicts and drug dealers. Prostitutes are likely to have daughters who follow in their footsteps. If a prostitute has a son, he is inclined to imitate what he has been accustomed to seeing, thus treating women with very little respect.

When a man neglects his role as a father, his son is more than likely to do the same, and the spirit of Abandonment will continue its work down that family lineage. If this father has a daughter, she is more likely to look for love in all the wrong places, in an unconscious effort to fill the absence of her father. In doing this, she begins a new cycle of generational curses.

Though generational curses can skip a generation, this does not mean they no longer exist. What it means is that you must study or examine the situations in your life and the life of your family closely and be willing to accept the possibility that a curse may be present.

When children become accustomed to seeing their parents or grandparents behave in a certain manner, they begin to display these same characteristics. They then begin their journey down that road of "life as normal."

Many end up believing that there is no hope, and they accept their fate without a second thought.

It amazes me that we somehow find solace in accepting the labels "you are just like your momma" or "I am just like my daddy."

Are our destinies predetermined by our parents and our upbringing?

In the inner city, or what many would call the hood or ghetto, my destiny was waiting. As I applied the "skills" handed down to me by my parents, I was destined to hand down those same skills to my children.

I grew up seeing the drugs, sex, murder, anger, alcohol, witchcraft, adultery, fornication, homosexuality, and ultimately *death.* This was life as normal for me.

Today countless young people are growing up in similar environments, and it is only by God's grace will they be able to come out of it. Sadly, without experiencing a better alternative, many of these individuals will die an untimely death.
For me, that is heart wrenching.

The Beginning

My mother's biological mother committed suicide when my mom was about twelve years old. Shortly after her death, my mom and her siblings moved in with my mom's stepfather and his new wife. Within a short time, living in this new environment would prove to be detrimental for many, including me, even though I was not yet born.

When she was not yet a teenager, my mom was raped by one of her relatives. To her surprise, no one believed her when she told them about it. Fearing for her life and in an effort to save herself, she ran away from home.

Identify and Acknowledge

With nowhere to go, she began her life on the streets, where *Addiction* found her. It was not long before she became pregnant, and at the age of fourteen she gave birth to my sister. When she was sixteen, she gave birth to me. My mom was young, hurt, and now addicted to drugs. As for me and my sister, we were left to live with our step-grandparents.

As she was bound to the streets, there was nothing left of my mom. Satan made sure of this. And since he had my mom, he was confident that he would have me too.

Dreaming for More

I remember growing up wanting more out of life than what I was accustomed to seeing. I would often visualize having a large family and would often say to myself, "When I have children, I am going to be there for them. When I become a mother, I am going to take care of my children like a real mother should."

But would I ever have children? This question plagued me because even though I hoped that I would not fall into the same traps as those before me, I also heard loud voices telling me that I would be dead by the age of eighteen.

A Reflection

At the age of twelve, I ran away from my step-grandparents' home. I left because of the physical and mental abuse, the drugs and alcohol, and the different sexual lifestyles that were played out day after day, right before my eyes.

I ran away with nowhere to go and no one to go to. Between the ages of twelve and fifteen, I ended up in several foster and group homes. Whenever I had the opportunity, I would run away from them as well. Filled with anger and wanting more out of life than what I was experiencing, I began looking for love in all the wrong places in an unconscious effort to fill the absence of the love I did not receive from a mother or father.

Searching for Love

Every person desires to be unconditionally loved and accepted. At a very young age, I began my quest to acquire both. I believed that if I had money, everything that was missing from my life would come.

I was young, and the lifestyle that I lived was very attractive. This was a lifestyle that I played up by going to the nail and hair salon every week. I would often shop at upscale boutiques and drive expensive cars. There was nothing for me to worry about; I had it all—or so I thought.

Identify and Acknowledge

From the outside it looked like I had it all together. I was a so-called "ghetto superstar," but there was definitely no stardom in what was going on inside of me.

The truth? I had nothing—nothing but an empty life, which was starting to look more and more like my childhood. It was a few years later and I was now a single mother with five children. I began to reflect on life and the future of my children. The more I reflected the more I found myself becoming increasingly terrified of what their lives might become.

What would I do about this new revelation?

And His Name Was Cain

Before I answer that question, let's take a look at the life of a man named Cain. I believe we can get a greater understanding of how generational curses work by observing this man's life and lineage.

Beginning in chapter four of Genesis, the first book in the Bible, is an account of Cain's life. Cain had a brother named Abel, whom he killed because God accepted Abel's offering but not his own.

But was this really why Cain killed his brother?

What we tend to see on the natural level is often due to something much deeper and at times much more sinister than we

would like to admit. When we begin to look at situations more closely, we will start to see the undercurrents that cause the tsunamis. These undercurrents are often warning signs that should not be ignored.

Cain's story continues: "Why are you so angry?" the Lord asked Cain. "Why do you look so dejected? You will be accepted if you do what is right. But if you refuse to do what is right, then watch out! Sin is crouching at your door, eager to control you. But you must subdue it and be its master."

The New Life Version (NLV) of the Bible records it like this:

"...If you do not do well, sin is waiting to destroy you. Its desire is to rule over you, but you must rule over it." (Genesis 4:6-7)

God was letting Cain know that he was not accepted and that he really needed to check himself before things got out of hand.

God saw that there was something more going on the inside Cain. God said, "You will be accepted if you do what is right." This was before Cain killed his brother.

God loves us so much that He will warn us in an effort to prevent us from making grave mistakes. He often gives us another chance to get it right, as He did with Cain.

Cain was at a point in his life where he was required to make an important decision. What would he do? Would he listen and obey God's instruction, or would he respond the same way his father did?

Cain's Father

Adam was Cain's father, and Adam had disobeyed God by eating from the tree of the Knowledge of Good and Evil when God commanded him not to. Both of Cain's parents disobeyed God and both came under specific curses.

Cain, Adam's son, was to bring the first of his offering before God; instead, he brought what he wanted in the way he wanted to bring it, instead of what was required by God.

God stated, "You will be accepted." The *you* meant this was about the heart behind the action and not the action alone. It was about the motive behind the giving of the offering.

How did Cain respond to his second opportunity?

He refused! He refused to change direction. He refused to bring God an offering, and he committed premeditated murder. He convinced his brother to go to the field with him, where he eventually killed him.

Cain killed his brother, but it did not stop there.

God asked Cain, "Where is your brother? Where is Abel?" Cain arrogantly responded, saying,

> *"I don't know. Am I my brother's guardian?" [NLV says, "Am I my brother's keeper."] But the Lord said, "What have you done? Listen! Your brother's blood cries out to me from*

the ground! Now you are cursed and banished from the ground, which has swallowed your brother's blood. No longer will the ground yield good crops for you, no matter how hard you work! From now on you will be a homeless wanderer on the earth." Cain replied to the Lord, "My punishment is too great for me to bear! You have banished me from the land and from your presence; you have made me a homeless wanderer, anyone who finds me will kill me!" (Genesis 4:9-14)

Cain displayed no remorse for his actions. He didn't care that he had rebelled against God or that he had murdered his brother. He was concerned only about how the consequences of his actions affected him.

If you follow the lineage of Cain, you will see that the curses Cain came under (because of his actions) affected the generations that came after him.

Imagine generation after generation being cursed before they were born—cursed not because of their actions but because of the actions of an individual that came before them, one they would never meet.

I Only Heard about My Ancestor Cain

After God informed Cain about the consequences of his actions, Cain moved on with his life. He settled in the land of Nod, which means "wandering," and he started a family. Cain had a son named Enoch, and he built a city and named it after his son.

Cain was enjoying his new life, and everything was going well—or so it seemed. Soon after, Cain's lineage began and so did the generational curses.

Identify and Acknowledge

First, Enoch had no relationship with God. Irad was Enoch's son, and he had no relationship with God. Irad had Mehujael, Mehujael had Methushael, and Methushael had Lamech. Lamech committed murder, married two women, and he, too, had no relationship with God. Lamech appeared to be more arrogant and rebellious than Cain, so much so that he summoned his two wives and mocked God, saying,

> *"Adah and Zillah, hear my voice. Listen to me, you wives of Lamech. I have killed a man who attacked me. If someone who kills Cain is punished seven times, then the one who kills me will be punished seventy-seven times!"* (Genesis 4:23-24)

Cain came under three specific curses—spiritual, mental, and physical—which were passed down to the next generations.

1. The Spiritual Curse

Cain's lineage had no relationship with God. They had no relationship with the One who created them in His image. They could have had a relationship with God, because their ancestor Adam did. Despite the fact that Adam sinned and suffered the consequences of his actions, he still taught his children (Cain, Abel, and Seth) about God and about the greatness of God. This spoke volume.

Adam disobeyed God by eating from the tree after God commanded him not to. He came under a curse because of his own actions, yet he taught his children about God and the greatness of God.

Not having a relationship with the One who created you results in a life of no value. The One who brought you into existence knows how and why you were created and what is needed for you to live a fulfilled and purposeful life.

If you have no relationship with God, you can never be whole or complete, no matter how hard you try. There are no substitutes for being in an intimate and personal relationship with your Father, God, for in this relationship we are complete.

To be under a spiritual curse is a dangerous place to be. When we are not in a true relationship with our Creator God by way of Jesus Christ, we try anything to find satisfaction, anything to be accepted, and anything to know true love. We go down a lot of dangerous roads—all in an attempt to gain what we can get only when we are in a right relationship with God through Christ Jesus. All other roads are dead ends.

Adam understood that his actions caused him to come under a curse—not the actions of God. Despite coming under a curse, Adam chose to teach his children about the God he knew. He taught them how to bring a gift, an offering that would be acceptable to God.

When Cain started his family, he taught his children about God, but what he taught them was far different from what Adam taught him. Adam taught Cain and Abel (and later Seth) about the goodness of God, while Cain taught his children how to mock and disobey God.

This is seen clearly in Lamech, who was in the seventh generation from Adam and who operated on a higher level of arrogance and disrespect than Cain. This shows how a curse that is initiated by our own willingness to sin weighs more heavily on the generations that come after us. Curses multiply!

Before we go any further, let's discuss Adam a little more. The sin of Adam and Eve (the mother and father of Cain, Abel, and Seth), which was their disobedience to God's instruction, was what brought sin into the world. In the unseen realm (spiritual realm), the seed of sin was deposited into their children.

Instead of living in sin and accepting a sin filled life, Adam did his best to make it right by demonstrating his love for God and by teaching his children about God. It was then up to his children to uproot any curse handed down to them from their parents. Adam's sons were born in this order: Cain then Abel then Seth.

Abel did what was right and unfortunately was killed at the hands of his brother for doing so. Seth did what was right. Cain did not. Seth was the third child who was born after Abel had died. It was in Seth's lineage, where the people began to worship the Lord by name, according to Genesis 4:26.

All three were raised by the same father and mother; two did right before God, but one did not.

Why did two of the brothers do what was right and one did not?

Why did two of the brothers do what was right and one did not? It is evident that their actions revealed the condition of their hearts. Abel and Seth took responsibility for their lives, while Cain did not. Abel and Seth refused to live under a curse. Cain, on the other hand, was full of rebellion, selfishness, and pride. He thought it was all about him, but as we have seen already, it wasn't.

2. The Mental Curse

Merriam Webster's Dictionary defines *wander* as to move about aimlessly, without a fixed course, and to lose normal mental contact. I am under the impression that Cain was dealing with the spirit of pride and jealousy. Instead of submitting to God and dealing with his heart issues, he yielded to temptation and sinned by killing his brother. Sin then became his master.

Remember, God warned Cain that sin was crouching at his door, waiting to master him, but he must subdue and master it. *Sin was waiting to control Cain.* He gave in, and therefore he came under the curse of a wanderer, a vagabond, a nomad, a drifter. When God told him about the curse he had come under, his response was "My punishment is too great for me to bear!" His response suggests that he was already under a curse before God told him about the consequences of his actions. There was no remorse or repentance from Cain, and now sin had become the dominating force in his life.

Six generations later, the curse that Cain was under became more evident. It was magnified in the life of Lamech.

When we sin, we do not have the freedom of determining the price that has to be paid for that sin or who else will have to pay

the price. The only decision we get to make is whether or not to give into temptation and sin.

3. The Physical Curse

Lamech was the first man mentioned in the Bible who had two wives. *A man under a curse was the first polygamist.* God is a God of order, and He places value on men and women alike. Men are not higher than women, and women are not higher than men, for it is God who said that He pours out His Spirit on all mankind: men, women, the young, and the old.

God's original design for marriage was that there be one man and one woman given to one another in the union of marriage. As the two become one in marriage, they would multiply physically and rule and reign in life. When their children grow up and marry, the men would love and honor their wives; their wives would respect and honor them; and they both would submit themselves one to another. This is the correct process of multiplication.

Having more than one spouse is a curse and is against the ordinance of God.

Therefore doth a man leave his father and his mother, and hath cleaved unto his wife [singular], and they have become one flesh.
(Genesis 2:24)

Anything other than this is not one flesh and is a curse.

Lamech had no respect for his wives. This was displayed in the poem he wrote: "*Hear my voice; you wives of Lamech, listen to what I say.*" This was far from the tone Adam took when God gave him Eve. *"Then the Lord God said, 'It is not good for the man to be alone. I will make a helper who is just right for him'"* (Genesis 2:18). Adam responded to the gift God had given him and he said, "*At last!... This one is bone from my bone, and flesh from my flesh! She will be called 'woman' because she was taken from 'man'*" (Genesis 2:23).

Sin Masters

The totality of a person is his or her body, soul (mind, will, and emotions), and spirit. The curses that Cain came under encompassed that totality.

God created man from the ground, but man did not come alive until God breathed the breath of life, or His Spirit, into him.

If one does not have the Spirit of God, what is the spirit that is giving him life?

Cain was a wanderer, or in today's terminology, he was insane. This was the curse on his *soul.*

The *body* is the temple of God, and God says for us not to defile it. The marrying of two spouses is the curse on the body and the family structure. Marriage and family was created by God.. God values each person equally, and when a home is one of polygamy, there is no equal value given. It can never be a happy home, where there is peace, unconditional love, joy, and value for one another. There would be perversions of all sorts. The children and their children's children will all be affected.

Sin is crouching at our door, but we must master it; otherwise, it will master us.

One of the scariest factors about Cain and those who followed consciously or unconsciously in his footsteps were their deaths. Sin may feel good for a moment, but the eternal consequences are to great to bear.

We all face one important question: When this life ends, what's next?

The Revelation Required My Response

I was determined to do better and be better than those I grew up seeing, no matter what. The truth? I was destined to die a horrific death; I was destined to go to hell, and I was preparing my children for that same destiny. Why? If I was to be honest with myself, my life was no different from what I grew up seeing. It was a little prettier, not as obvious (or so I thought), and maybe a little more flamboyant. But it was the same pattern being repeated, and I was the one living it out—right before my children's eyes.

It's interesting how Satan sells the same lie but in a different package. The image looked prettier to me, but the curses were the same.

The same game ends up being played by each generation, with the same results. The only difference is the players.

How would I respond to what I was seeing?

Chapter Two
The Heart

I began to reflect on life and what it was really about. During that time of reflection, I came to terms with what I needed to do, and that was to accept the fact that I needed a new heart.

If we plan on reaching our destiny, we must be completely honest with ourselves. We must learn to swallow that bitter pill of truth. I did.

My heart had been conditioned to darkness, and its overall state was horrific. I did not have a heart of God, and to make matters worse, I did not grow up in an environment where God was important (or so it seemed). The closest I came to knowing about God was seeing people go to church on Sunday and live the street life the rest of the week. When I say that my heart was conditioned to darkness, what I mean is that it was corrupt, evil, lustful, and selfish. There was no good to be found in it.

The human heart is the most deceitful of all things, and desperately wicked. Who really knows how bad it is? (Jeremiah 17:9-10)

My heart was incapable of loving unconditionally, and it was limited to my understanding of love. There was nothing in me that knew what true unconditional love meant. Even though I had children, I had experienced only worldly and conditional love. So that was what I understood. When my children were younger, it was about me proving that I could be a better parent. It wasn't about their hearts and their destinies, because I had no idea of what hearts and destinies were.

As my children grew up, it was about their behavior and grades. The more they behaved, the more affection I showed them. That's conditional! Our level of love is based on our capacity for and capability to love. Without new hearts, we are incapable of demonstrating and experiencing unconditional love.

I did not experience the unconditional love of a mother or the unconditional love of a father. I did not experience unconditional love nor did I have the capability of offering it. Therefore I became a master at conditional love. It was like this: give me what I ask for, and I will give you my definition of love.

How could I love my children unconditionally with the state of my heart? How could I love anyone else, for that matter? I couldn't. I couldn't love myself unconditionally because by natural means my love was limited. My love for myself was based on the amount of material possessions I acquired. The more I acquired, the more I "loved" myself. The more I outperformed others, the better physical shape I was in, the prettier I was, the more skin I revealed—the more I loved myself. The reality was that the more attention and acceptance (good or bad) I received from the masses, the more I was able to accept myself. But the feeling of being accepted lasted only for a few moments.

A Day of Heartache

I remember that day so vividly. It was a late summer afternoon when I fell to my knees on the bathroom floor and cried out to a God I did not know. I remember saying, "God, if You are real show Yourself to me." What I was really asking was for God to love me, for God to show me His definition of love. I was tired of performing, tired of wearing the mask, tired of the artificial love. I was longing for a love that would fill the depths of my soul, a love that would accept me for who and how I was, a love that would never abandon me.

I believe this was the lowest point of my life, because I had everything from the world's perspective, but there was a massive emptiness inside me that words cannot describe. That emptiness filled every fiber of my being. I felt that if the emptiness wasn't filled with what it was meant to be filled with, I would rather die.

There are many who go through life trying to fill this same emptiness with other things like sex, drugs, position, and power—just to end up worse off than before and destroyed in the process.

The only thing that can fill this emptiness is the love of God. I am a living witness that nothing—no thing—can fill this emptiness but the love of God through His Son, Jesus. Nothing else! Once you have felt it, once you have tasted it (for real), you will do whatever it takes to keep it.

About three weeks after that episode on the bathroom floor, my neighbor came by to ask if I wanted to attend a Bible study. God has perfect timing! If she would have asked me at any other time before that, I would have cursed her out. Me and church people? Absolutely not!

As I stated before, I did not grow up in church, but I watched those who did, and I saw that many were not sold out on the God they professed. Most would talk as if they were better than me, but at night, the real person showed up. Be around church people, me?

But this time, it was different. I gladly accepted the invitation; I was so excited to learn about God that the thought of being around church people didn't bother me at all.

True Love Revealed

Bible study time came, and my children and I went next door. To my surprise, there was an elderly white woman conducting the lesson that day. I do not usually use color to describe people, but for illustration purposes I must. I need you to see (in your heart) what God showed me that day. After observing this woman for a little while, I noticed that she walked with a cane, and her legs and arms were extremely swollen. But this did not seem to deter her. It was clear that she was there to love on anyone who would receive the love she had to offer, and she painlessly broke the Bible down in a way that we all could understand.

There was something so amazing about her, though her body was visibly failing, the tenacity she had outshined all of that. Her love for God was demonstrated in her love for people and she showed special attention to the children who attended the study without their parents.

After the lesson, refreshments were served. We hung around getting to know one another, and it was a wonderful day—just wonderful!

Unknown to me then, God was answering my prayer, "God, if You are real, show Yourself to me." For the first time in my life, I saw a demonstration of unconditional love through this lovely woman. She gave her time and her energy, and with a genuine love embraced us all—young and old, no matter the color. She was so willing to share her love with us, those who may not have ever encountered it.

After attending the first Bible study, I felt a greater sense of emptiness; yet at the same time there was hope rising within me. I began to look forward to attending Bible study more than I looked forward to anything else. I wanted to learn more about this Jesus they were teaching about.

The study was every week for about two months. When it ended, I began attending church. In my mind, I needed to know that God was *it.* I needed to know that He would never leave me, that He would love me and give me purpose. I needed to know that He was what I had been searching for all along.

I desired something true, real, and permanent to take place in my life, and it came when I accepted Jesus into my heart. I gave my old heart to Jesus and accepted His heart, even though I had no idea what it all meant.

If you confess with your mouth that Jesus is Lord and believe in your heart that God raised him from the dead, you will be saved. (Romans: 10:9)

I confessed with my mouth that Jesus was Lord and believed with my heart that God raised Him from the dead. But I still wondered if I was saved.

I am a visual learner, so for me to grasp and understand things I need to be able to see things in my mind's eye. I asked, "Why not just believe; why must I believe with my heart?" God was saying that I must open my mouth to make the confession and believe in my heart (the belief must go deeper than the mind) to receive the heart of Jesus. Believing with the heart is the only way for the heart transplant to take place.

God wanted to give me the heart of his Son, Jesus, which loves unconditionally, and only by receiving His heart could I be saved. In other words, I would now be in a personal relationship with a loving and holy God.

Another question I had was "Saved? Saved from what? What would I be saved from or saved to?" There were so many questions and no one to ask. I could not talk with my friends or family, and I couldn't see myself talking with church people, so who would help me? I was looking for someone who came from where I was coming from, who had gone through what I was going through, who could answer my questions. But there was no one. There were a lot of questions and no one to ask. *What? Ask God?* If I were to ask God all of these questions, how would He answer? And if He answered, how would I know that it was Him answering?

When you leave the old life behind and follow Jesus, there will be a lot of questions. You will need immediate help to avoid going

back to that old way of living. Getting connected in a local Bible based church and Bible study class is a great place to start.

There were so many questions, and no one to ask. I began to think that I was losing my mind but from God's point of view, I was on my way to stepping into my destiny.

Chapter Three
The Eyes

I accepted Jesus as my Lord. I confessed He was the Son of God and believed in my heart that God raised Him from the dead. And I received my new heart.

I was now saved, and I thought everything would get better, but to my surprise everything got worse. Everything around me began to fall apart. I felt sick to my stomach every day, as if I was dying. "What is this? What is happening to me? Somebody help me, please help me!" My life was spinning out of control, and everything I valued was being destroyed right before my eyes. My sixty-inch flat-screen television broke. Soon after the microwave did too. Then it was the washer and dryer. The worst was my car, which was on its second round of repairs.

Even though everything I owned was breaking down, I refused to stress over money. Money was never an issue for me, because I could always get it, multiply it, and keep it. I was confident in my abilities to multiply anything I set my hands to, but things were heading in a totally different direction.

The Eyes

"You don't understand now what I am doing, but someday you will." (John 13:7)

During this period, when everything appeared to be falling apart, I was without a job. It was OK though, because I had money. I had received a nice severance package, and I was not in a hurry to find a job. I decided early on that I would take my time to position myself properly.

Blinded by Pride

I am not sure why I didn't see all the devastation that was lurking ahead of me. It is likely that my pride blinded me. There is no other reason to explain why I was not prepared for what lay ahead.

As I stated, my car was on its second round of repairs. The first time it was the engine; the second time it was a computer chip. But the third time—yes, before the second round of repairs was completed, the car was stolen from the repair shop. And this was after I had paid for all the repairs.

Before anything started to go wrong with the car, I'd had metallic tint put on the windows. I purchased custom rims and brand-new tires. And after all the money I spent on the car, it was stolen from the repair shop. Yes, from the repair shop! I couldn't believe it. It had to be a bad dream. This could not be happening to me. Who would steal a car from a repair shop?! Well, someone did, and the police report confirmed it.

I was still blind with pride, because there was more to come and I just could not see what was before me. I should have slowed down to try to analyze what was happening, but I didn't. I couldn't. My pride and arrogance were too blinding.

I wasted money repeatedly. Why? Because I was so confident in my ability to make money that nothing else mattered. I was a master at it, so who or what could stop me?

I started looking for another vehicle and was shocked when I was told that I didn't qualify for a loan because the car that was stolen was showing up as an open line of credit. It would remain there until the insurance and car company worked things out. The dealers weren't willing to give me another loan because I didn't have a job. So I thought, *OK, I'll just rent vehicles until the situation blows over.* This was stupid. I spent everything I had on car rentals. I did all this to maintain an image, since I wanted to look the best, drive the best, and have the best. Oh, and by the way, I was now saved.

I began to feel a fog over me. It was as if I couldn't see at all, let alone think. My whole life was spiraling out of control. I needed a car, and the only way to get a car was to have a job. I was not ready to work, because I was in the process of planning my new life. There I was, in a situation that I was not at all accustomed to. I had nothing. I needed money, and I needed money fast.

Pictures began to flash through my mind of how I used to make money, and I could hear a voice saying, "Pick up the phone; you know how to get it. Go get it." Money was the god of my life. Would I yield to what I was hearing and seeing, even though I was now saved?

This is where I began to pray for God to help me. My back was against the wall. In a moment of what I see as sanity, I looked up to the heavens and told God that I needed His help. I did not want to go back to that old life—I knew the consequences. I decided in my heart that forward was the only way for me to go. There was no other choice, no matter how hard it got.

Reality Revealed

It was clear what I had to do and that was to get a job. I would leave home each morning, drop the kids off to school, and go look for a job until it was time to pick them up. Looking for a job was a full-time job. Then suddenly a door opened.. I was offered a job at a catalog company after a background and credit check was completed.

About a day before I was to start this new job, I got a call and was told that they had to withdraw the offer of employment because my credit score wasn't high enough. I was devastated. The job would have offered the amount of pay I was accustomed to. I was back to nothing. Now what?

Again I began to search for a job. About two days later, I applied for a position at a credit card company. I did not want to work there, but it was the only company that was paying close to what I needed. A few years prior, I had worked in their collections department during the Christmas season to earn extra money. it was not a place I wanted to go on a regular basis.

I had no choice. I went and applied. To my surprise, after I did all the required testing, I was granted an immediate interview. Everything was going well until the man said, "The only thing we have to do now is a credit check."

I was like, "What? Check my credit?!"

"Yes, check your credit. This is a credit card company, we have to run your credit."

I said, "OK." I had no choice; I needed a job.

When the man went to run my credit, I was in the lobby praying and asking God to remove all stains from my credit record. A short time later, he came back and said, "Great, you got the job."

I was dumbfounded, so I asked him about my credit.

He said, "It's perfect."

I was at a loss for words. I had just been declined a job that I really wanted because of my credit, and here this man was telling me my credit was perfect. Still in shock, I accepted the position and thanked God for what He had done. I was confused, but at least I now had a job.

Never underestimate what God is doing. It may seem strange to you, but if you keep pressing forward, God will open doors that will lead you into your destiny. Accepting this job allowed me to meet my husband.

Seeing Vain Things

On the first day of work, I walked into the orientation room with an attitude as if to say, "People, please, don't say anything to me, because I just might say what is on my mind." I can say, "My life was jacked up," a thousand times over, and it would not describe what I was going through at the time. I accepted Jesus as my Savior and Lord, but I was still messed up and now more confused than ever.

I walked into the orientation room late, and as I was standing in the back of the room, looking for a seat, a man who looked all proper said with a heavy British accent, "Take a seat. You are late." Everything within me wanted to curse him out, but since the entire class was now looking at me, I sat down next to him.

After the instructor regained the attention of the class, he stated, "Now turn to the person next to you and introduce yourself." I introduced myself, and then it was his turn. His name was Sola Adewunmi, and because of his accent, I asked where he was from. He said Nigeria.

Now here is this man dressed all proper, speaking with a British accent, and the first thing I thought was, *Yep, he got money.* And since he was trying to talk to me, I would gladly take it. In my mind, all he could do for me was pay my bills. Even though my heart had changed, my vision had not.

Turn away my eyes from beholding vanity (idols and idolatry); and restore me to vigorous life and health in your ways. (Psalms 119:37)

Everything out of my old heart was evil. How could this evil still exist within me when I now had a new heart? This was possible because salvation didn't mean I was going to be changed overnight. It meant I was now in a right relationship with God through Christ Jesus. I would have to learn how to live a new life with a new heart, eyes, body, and mind.

Seeing Through the Eyes of God

All the thoughts I had about this man were far from who he was. I thought he had money; he did not. He walked with royalty and he talked like he had great wealth; he did not (at least from an earthly standpoint). I was still looking with my natural eyes, but God was calling me to see through the new vision He had given me. I was to look at Sola through the eyes of Jesus. What would I see?

O taste and see that the Lord [our God] is good! Blessed (happy, fortunate, to be envied) is the man who trusts and takes refuge in Him. (Psalms 34:8)

Since we consider and look not to the things that are seen but to the things that are unseen; for the things that are visible are temporal (brief and fleeting), but the things that are invisible are deathless and everlasting. (2 Corinthians 4:18)

I began to focus my eyes on what God saw. It is like a person who has been blind from birth, and when that person is given sight, they have to refocus their eyes to see clearly.

And instantly something like scales fell from [Saul's] eyes, and he recovered his sight. Then he arose and was baptized. (Acts 9:18)

I began to see that Sola would be my mentor, my future husband, my earthly teacher, and my mighty man of valor, and I would be his helpmate. A man made in God's image was what I began to see.

Sola knew who he was, and he knew who his Father was, and that was why he walked the way he did.

We can never live a new life if we are unable to see clearly. Imagine walking through life in complete darkness. Even worse, imagine walking through life in complete darkness not knowing you are in complete darkness.

"The eye is the lamp of the body. If your eyes are healthy, your whole body will be full of light. But if your eyes are unhealthy, your whole body will be full of darkness. If then the light within you is darkness, how great is that darkness!"(Matthew 6:22-23)

When I focused on the Word of God, it told me who I was to God and in God. I meditated on God's Word because I was desperate—extremely desperate—to live beyond what I had known my entire life. My desperation led me into the presence of God through praying and reading His Word.

Prior to this I did not know how to read a Bible, but my passion led me to learn. The time I spent alone with God was very exciting. I was reading His Word, meditating on it, and I began to believe every word. I began to see myself beyond my circumstances, and I had hope that things would change for the good.

Then Jesus said, "Did I not tell you that if you believe, you will see the glory of God?" (John 11: 40)

Your eyes saw my unformed body. All the days ordained for me were written in your book before one of them came to be.

How precious to me are your thoughts, God! How vast is the sum of them! (Psalms 139:16-17)

So do not fear, for I am with you; do not be dismayed, for I am your God. I will strengthen you and help you; I will uphold you with my righteous right hand. (Isaiah 41:10)

Jesus answered, "It is written: 'People do not live on bread alone, but on every word that comes from the mouth of God.'" (Matthew 4:4)

"Daughter, be encouraged! Your faith has made you well." (Matthew 9:22)

Chapter Four
The Body

My vision was changing, but my circumstances were not. All the appliances in my home were now broken, and I no longer had a car or money to buy one.

I started remembering how I had accumulated all the things that had broken, and I realized they were given to me in prior relationships. Money? I had made money the god of my life. And for the first time since I could remember, I couldn't get it, I couldn't keep it, and I couldn't multiply it. It was all gone, as if it were sand falling through my fingers.

The prayer I prayed that day on the bathroom floor a few months back was still being answered. "God, if You are real, show Yourself to me." It started with seeing an elderly woman share her love of Jesus with others. It was meeting a *real* man of God, and then it was the removing and destroying of all the things that had been given to me in prior relationships. The biggest of them all was the dismantling of the money god I had exalted.

Another Door Opens

The credit card company where Sola and I met was unable to provide me with a shift that coincided with my parental responsibilities, so I had to look for another job. I was a single mother who wasn't getting help from anyone. In addition to the schedule, it was hard for me to accept a job that paid less than what I desired, because I had a lifestyle to maintain. But God had a different plan.

I was back on the road, looking for a job. I submitted my resume to several companies, but no one called me back. I couldn't understand why no was calling me, I knew I was qualified for most of the positions. What was I going to do? My unemployment was running out. I became amazed at the number of circumstances that gave way to opportunities for me to turn back to that old way of living.

Then a phone call came; it was someone responding to my resume. I was given an opportunity to interview for a receptionist position and was so excited about someone calling me back that I forgot to ask about the pay. Even though I considered a receptionist position beneath my qualifications, I was just happy to have someone call me for a job.

I interviewed the next day, and everything went great.

The following day the company called me back and thanked me for the interview but noted they had offered the position to someone else. I was shocked.

Over the next few days, the phone did not ring, and I was once again back at that point of desperation for a job. But I still had a certain amount of pay in mind. The job search continued, and no door opened. Not one.

Great! Another phone call! It was from the company I had interviewed with; apparently it had not worked out with the person they had originally offered the position to. The job was mine if I was still interested. Yes, I was interested, and I accepted the position, despite the pay. It was the only door that opened for me, and I knew I had to step through it. God used this place and position to strip me of the confidence I had in myself and to propel me into my destiny.

Complete Submission

Sola and I got married about nine months after we met, and I can truly say that God used him in a mighty way to disrobe me even further of all that I thought I was. *Who am I?* I began to ask myself on a regular basis. I wasn't looking the same, thinking the same, acting the same. Who am I?

At times everything was a complete blur, as if life was not real. There were also times when a little hope gleamed from inside. It uttered, "Even though things are completely chaotic, you will be better off than you were." I can't explain it; I somehow knew I would be better off than I was, even if it didn't look or feel like it.

There was no turning back for me. The only way I would be able to move forward would be with God's help and if I completely surrendered myself to His will (which is accepting His Lordship). I knew that if I was going to leave the old me behind, I could not play with this relationship I now had with God. I had to be real and walk straight, because that old life was waiting for me to come back. If I dared to go back, complete darkness would consume me, my destiny as well as my children and their destiny.

There was no turning back. I would physically die if I went back to the old way of living, and I could not fathom my children living a life like the one I once lived. I remember praying, "God, whatever I need to do to walk right with you, show me—and I will do it."

God was telling me that there were two sides to the cross.

Many accept Jesus as their Savior, but deny Him as Lord. They continue to live the same life they lived before accepting His salvation. They live in continuous sin and defeat and often utter the words "I'm saved and I am going to heaven." Only a few accept the Lordship of Jesus.

"Go in through the narrow gate, because the gate to hell is wide and the road that leads to it is easy, and there are many who travel it." (Matthew 7: 13)

When you are under Jesus's Lordship, you die to self, you are stripped of the world, and you are transformed into the image and likeness of Christ. It is under the Lordship that we are to live life, for this is where abundance flows.

"Are you ready to allow Jesus to be the Lord of your life?" There was no other choice for me. I am a person who cannot live with Jesus being Savior only, for I know there was more that took place at the cross.

In His death, we die to sin and we have salvation; in His resurrection, we have life.

I knew that having part of Jesus and not all of Jesus would not work for me; I knew I would literally have to die to myself. It's like accepting healing, but only taking half of the prescribed medication. You may live a little longer, and the symptoms might go away for a little while, but the sickness remains.

God said, "Accepting Jesus as Lord will cost you your life." *Accepting Jesus as Lord will cost me my life?* I did not understand then what this meant, but I do now. God was not referring to the same death that I was thinking of. I was thinking of a physical death, meaning if I stayed in the relationship with Jesus as my Savior only—not as my Savior and Lord—I was certain to go back to the old way of living, where a detestable, physical death awaited. I now understand sin and the power of sin, and I understand that the only way for me to win is to walk with Jesus as my Lord.

Satan needs us to give him something (our willingness to walk in sin) for him to legally have a right to our life and the life of our family.

Satan has a plan of destruction bigger than we think. It may appear that he wants one thing, but his plan is to take *everything*. He enters through the door of sin to take it all.

"The thief comes only to steal and kill and destroy."
(John 10:10)

Many think that sin is harmless, that a little sin won't hurt anyone. That is what Satan wants us to believe. Sin is harmless, and it won't hurt? Who are we kidding? It is a death trap. Jesus died a death so gruesome that his body was marred beyond recognition. Jesus knew the price of sin and paid the ultimate price for all to be free. So why would I continue in sin when I understand what He has done for me and what it will cost me?

The only way for us to win is to break the generation curses from our lives and from the lives of our children. We must completely surrender our will to God by accepting the Lordship of Jesus.

God was referring to the death of my old self, which means dying to all that I believed, dying to my way of thinking, dying to my plans and my dreams. If I accepted Jesus as my Lord, Cherlene would die—but it would be the first time she lived!

> *Therefore, since we have these promises, dear friends, let us purify ourselves from everything that contaminates body and spirit, perfecting holiness out of reverence for God.*
> *(2 Corinthian 7:1)*

The Prunning Process

I went through seven years of great pain and anguish. Imagine dying every day for seven consecutive years. Imagine all that you knew, all that you were, and all that you thought you were,-stripped away. Things you liked to watch on television you could no longer watch. Music you used to listen to you could not listen to anymore. And if you did, it would make you sick to your stomach. Places you used to go, people you used to hang out with—God was saying, "No, I need you away from all direct and indirect forms of contamination."

During these seven years I remember feeling horrible. Some days were OK, but the majority of the time I felt horrible. The only way for me to describe my life during those seven years was as being placed in a blender and that blender was on full blast.

My insides were always out of whack, and this "pruning" process that God was taking me through was extremely painful.

The way I wore my hair and style of dress was no longer acceptable, for when I looked in the mirror it gave me such an uneasy feeling. I was being stripped of the identity I had created for myself.

Wife? God had the perfect man for me, but was I willing to submit to his leadership and learn my role as a wife, honor him, esteem him, serve him? Mother? How could I be the mother I was created to be, when I wasn't raised by my own mother?

There were many nights I would fall asleep on the floor, crying. The pain of change was so great that all I could do was pray, cry, and pray some more until I fell asleep. Through the pain, I learned to call on the name of God, to hear from God, and to give my body as a sacrifice to God. I learned to serve God and others, and I learned to honor and fear God. I now knew what it meant to have Jesus as Savior and Lord.

What did it cost me? It cost me everything, and everything was definitely worth it.

> *As for you, the anointing you received from him remains in you, and you do not need anyone to teach you. But as his anointing teaches you about all things and as that anointing is real, not counterfeit—just as it has taught you, remain in him. (1 John 2:27)*

If someone claims, "I know God," but doesn't obey God's commandments, that person is a liar and is not living according to the truth. (1 John 2:4)

Those who say they live in God should live their lives as Jesus did. (1 John 2:6)

Chapter Five
The Power

This book is a blueprint designed to help you begin the process of stepping into your destiny. If you want more out of life, you must go through the process. When you do you will never be the same. Your new life is going to be great!

> *And without faith it is impossible to please God, because anyone who comes to him must believe that he exists and that he rewards those who earnestly seek him.*
> *(Hebrews 11:6)*

We have established that, first, we need a new heart. The reason we need a new heart is because our hearts (the hearts that we had since birth) are contaminated and are incapable of loving unconditionally. The only way to receive a new heart is when we accept Jesus Christ as Savior and Lord. Once we accept Jesus as Savior and Lord we become alive for the first time and are now in a right relationship with God.

The next step is learning how to see. Since our vision is naturally blurred and darkened by our life experiences, we need corrective lenses. Meditating on and believing the Word of God allows us to see ourselves and our lives the way God sees us. A person with a vision is powerful but, a person with blurred vision is destined to fail.

> *"Can one blind person lead another? Won't they both fall into a ditch?" (Luke 6:39)*

Meditating on the Word of God changes the way we think. As our thinking changes, we change.

> *And be not conformed to this world: but be ye transformed by the renewing of your mind, that ye may prove what is that good, and acceptable, and perfect, will of God. (Romans 12:2)*

In chapter four, we learned about the body and how we need to truly understand what lordship means and submit our lives completely over to the Lordship of Christ. Jesus is to be the Savior and Lord of our lives. We are to give our bodies as a living sacrifice to God and should no longer defile it with the old way of living. Our bodies now belong to a holy God who dwells inside us.

> *Therefore, brothers and sisters, we have an obligation—but it is not to the sinful nature, to live according to it. For if you live according to the sinful nature, you will die; but if by the Spirit you put to death the misdeeds of the body, you will live. (Romans 8:12-13)*

If our bodies are truly temples in which God dwells, why would we continue to treat our bodies the same way we did prior to His indwelling.

We must die

God requires that our bodies (lives) be given completely over to Him to be treated and used as He originally designed. Therefore, to get to that place where God has complete control over our bodies and life, the "old man" must die and the old junk must come out. The only way the old junk can come out is through a cleansing period. I call this the "pruning process."

Many people who accept Jesus Christ as Savior try to bypass the pruning process, because it is painful. It's painful to give up selfish habits, lust, and evil intentions. But every part of our old life must die so that God can live and move freely through us. Those who try to bypass this period of their walk with God end up never experiencing the ultimate intimate relationship God designed and they never fulfill their God ordained destiny.

All the attitudes, old ways of scheming, sin, and desires must die! This makes room for the holy God to have His way. Oh, how wonderful it is to be one with Christ, to be complete and fulfilled.

I noted earlier that my pruning process took seven long years and then some. Maybe if I had worked with God instead of against Him, this period would have been shorter. In those seven years I learned to go to God, because He was the only one who could teach me how to live. A deep intimate relationship developed, and I desired Him with a passion, so I began to seek Him daily.

When I went to my Father, the first thing out of my mouth was "Teach me how to live." Then I would begin to sing, "Teach me how to live, oh Lord, teach me how to live." The more I sang, the more I cried. "Teach me how to live, oh Lord. I need your eyes, Lord, your ears, Lord, your heart, Lord. Teach me how to live."

I remember learning everything through the time I spent alone in prayer and reading God's Word. I learned to pray by praying, I learned how to read the Bible by reading, I learned to wait by waiting, and I learned to worship by going through hardships while trusting God. And with the help of the Holy Spirit, I learned how to live. He is my power.

The pruning process is much easier when we are willing to yield to God and wait patiently while the process is being completed.

I praise the Lord for my pruning process. I am who I am today because of it. God had to burn all the infirmities and iniquities from my life, and He must do the same with you, if you want to become who you were created to be.

As I learned to sing, I also learned the power of the Holy Spirit. I don't remember the exact day when I was baptized in the Holy Spirit, but I do remember that it was at the early onset of the seven years. The Holy Spirit is the Spirit of God. He tells me to be quiet when I'm talking too much. He comforts me when I am experiencing hurt and rejection; He gives me strength to get through the most difficult times of life. And He teaches me. He is my helper.

But the Comforter, which is the Holy Ghost, whom the Father will send in my name, he shall teach you all things, and bring all things to your remembrance, whatsoever I have said unto you. (John 14:26)

I would have missed the greatest opportunity of knowing God on a much deeper and intimate level if I had not been willing to go through the fire that was designed to make me holy like my Father, God.

For us to walk into our destiny, we need to receive the Holy Spirit, He is our everyday power.

"But you will receive power when the Holy Spirit comes on you; and you will be my witnesses in Jerusalem, and in all Judea and Samaria, and to the ends of the earth." (Acts 1:8)

After they prayed, the place where they were meeting was shaken. And they were all filled with the Holy Spirit and spoke the word of God boldly. (Acts 4:31)

In the same way, the Spirit helps us in our weakness. We do not know what we ought to pray for, but the Spirit himself intercedes for us through wordless groans. And he who searches our hearts knows the mind of the Spirit, because the Spirit intercedes for God's people in accordance with the will of God. And we know that in all things God works for the good of those who love him, who have been called according to his purpose. (Romans 8:26-28)

Chapter Six
The Feet

To step into our destinies, we must be willing to step out of and away from our past. We must let it all go!

> *I do not consider that I have made it my own. But one thing I do: forgetting what lies behind and straining forward to what lies ahead, I press on toward the goal for the prize of the upward call of God in Christ Jesus. (Philippians 3:13–14)*

My past did not determine my future, and my future has no room for my past. I don't want to see it; it's gone, and it has no place for where God is taking me.

Stepping out of your past is going to cost you something; it may just cost you everything. But there is no greater cost than the cost Jesus paid on the cross for you and I.

> *"For God so loved the world that he gave his one and only Son, that whoever believes in him shall not perish but have eternal life. For God did not send his Son into the*

world to condemn the world, but to save the world through him."(John 3:16)

Eternal life with God and Christ Jesus is our ultimate destiny.

"Whoever believes in the Son has eternal life, but whoever rejects the Son will not see life, for God's wrath remains on them."(John 3:36)

You Must do Something

We must come to the full understanding that we need Jesus. There is no other way to reach our God-ordained destinies without first accepting the salvation that is made available only through Jesus Christ.

God is love, and everything He does is out of the love He has for humanity.

As I meditated on John 3:16, I learned that God gave His Son over to death itself, so that you and I can have a restored relationship with Him. That relationship, which was severed by the fall of man (through Adam and Eve), has been restored through Jesus, and one day we will spend eternity together with Him.

What is the most important commandment? Love.

"The most important one," answered Jesus, "is this: 'Hear, O Israel: The Lord our God, the Lord is one. Love the

Lord your God with all your heart and with all your soul and with all your mind and with all your strength. The second is this: 'Love your neighbor as yourself.' There is no commandment greater than these." (Mark 12:29-31)

God is Love. He created us in His image, and He gave His Son so that we could have a relationship (which he originally purposed) with Him. He requires that we love Him with everything we have, not because He needs anything from us but because He desires His children to be like Him. He desires to have a relationship with us.

All Scripture is God-breathed and is useful for teaching, rebuking, correcting and training in righteousness, so that all God's people may be thoroughly equipped for every good work. (2 Timothy 3:16-17)

When we give God *every* part of our life, we close the door on Satan. If we give God *some* areas of our life, Satan has open access for destruction.

God tells us to love Him, because while we love Him, we get to experience the greatest love one could ever imagine: His all-powerful, unlimited, and unconditional love.

"Love God with All Your Heart."

How can we love some and hate others? As humans, we have many prejudices that we carry and so much wickedness that comes from the depths of our heart. When we give our hearts to Jesus, we then live from His heart. What an impact we would make in this world if we all had the heart of Jesus!

Every prejudice we can imagine has been destroyed by Jesus.

There is neither Jew nor Gentile, neither slave nor free, nor is there male and female, for you are all one in Christ Jesus. (Galatians 3:28)

For there is no difference between Jew and Gentile—the same Lord is Lord of all and richly blesses all who call on him, for, "Everyone who calls on the name of the Lord will be saved." (Romans 10:12-13)

In the last days, God says, I will pour out my Spirit on all people. Your sons and daughters will prophesy, your young men will see visions, your old men will dream dreams. (Acts 2:17)

Everyone is equal and loved by God.

"Love God with All Your Soul."

Our soul is comprised of our mind, our will, and our emotions. Our natural thoughts are evil and lustful. If there was a screen that played our thoughts before everyone, what would be revealed? Exactly!

The Bible tells us to be transformed by the renewing of our minds. With our minds focused on God, we begin to have thoughts of who we were created to be. We love beyond our human understanding. Our thoughts are God's thoughts, and we are not self-seeking and self-exalting.

When we allow God to reign in our lives, giving everything over to Him, He uses our personalities to impact others and the world. Our mental and emotional state is in balance and is used for its original purpose. And our emotions do not control us; we control them.

"Love God with All Your Strength."

Strength means the capacity for exertion, endurance, or support; it is the power of a person or of God measured variously in terms, such as wealth, wisdom, military might, or physical power.

We utilize our strengths to gain the things of this world that will pass away. This means that we waste our strength and life on waste.

God is saying, love Him with all of you, and you will in turn have great gain now and for all eternity. We have been blinded by Satan and the things of this world, when the answer to our victory is simple. It is Jesus.

> *"The thief comes only to steal and kill and destroy; I have come that they may have life, and have it to the full." (John 10:10)*

Jesus is my Lord and my Savior. There is nothing more satisfying than going to Him, sitting at His feet, and worshiping Him. He is a wonderful Lord who has the best in store for us.

I have experienced countless breakthroughs and victories. I have eaten from the plate of freedom. I have tasted the miracles of God and have drunk from the cup of victory. But even greater than all these is the realization that I now know and understand the love of God. I know who I am and why I was created, and I am living on the second side of the cross in the Lordship of Jesus.

Nothing can fill the void of my life like the love of God. Every day I live with the expectancy that God is going to do something new. God is up to something every single day. His blessings are new each and every day.

I have broken the chains of generational curses, by the blood of Jesus. I was delivered by the blood of Jesus. I have been set free by the blood of Jesus. And I am walking out my God ordained destiny in the name of Jesus.

I am excited! I get excited because I know what being set free looks and feels like. Oh yes, I know the love of God, because He shows it to me. My past? It's gone! All gone! My destiny? I'm walking in it.

Accept Jesus as your Savior, and you will receive His heart and be in a right relationship with the Father. Accept His Lordship, and step into your destiny.

I leave you with the words of Apostle Paul:

Unity in the Body

Therefore I, a prisoner for serving the Lord, beg you to lead a life worthy of your calling, for you have been called by

God. Always be humble and gentle. Be patient with each other, making allowance for each other's faults because of your love. Make every effort to keep yourselves united in the Spirit, binding yourselves together with peace. For there is one body and one Spirit, just as you have been called to one glorious hope for the future. There is one Lord, one faith, one baptism, and one God and Father, who is over all and in all and living through all.

However, he has given each one of us a special gift through the generosity of Christ. That is why the Scriptures say,

"When he ascended to the heights,
he led a crowd of captives
and gave gifts to his people."

Notice that it says "he ascended." This clearly means that Christ also descended to our lowly world. And the same one who descended is the one who ascended higher than all the heavens, so that he might fill the entire universe with himself.

Now these are the gifts Christ gave to the church: the apostles, the prophets, the evangelists, and the pastors and teachers. Their responsibility is to equip God's people to do his work and build up the church, the body of Christ. This will continue until we all come to such unity in our faith and knowledge of God's Son that we will be mature in the Lord, measuring up to the full and complete standard of Christ.

Then we will no longer be immature like children. We won't be tossed and blown about by every wind of new teaching. We will not be influenced when people try to trick us with lies so clever they sound like the truth. Instead, we will speak the truth in love, growing in every way more and more like Christ, who is the head of his body, the church. He makes the whole body fit together perfectly. As each part does its own special work, it helps the other parts grow, so that the whole body is healthy and growing and full of love.

Living as Children of Light

With the Lord's authority I say this: Live no longer as the Gentiles do, for they are hopelessly confused. Their minds are full of darkness; they wander far from the life God gives because they have closed their minds and hardened their hearts against him. They have no sense of shame. They live for lustful pleasure and eagerly practice every kind of impurity.

But that isn't what you learned about Christ. Since you have heard about Jesus and have learned the truth that comes from him, throw off your old sinful nature and your former way of life, which is corrupted by lust and deception. Instead, let the Spirit renew your thoughts and attitudes. Put on your new nature, created to be like God—truly righteous and holy.

So stop telling lies. Let us tell our neighbors the truth, for we are all parts of the same body. And "don't sin by letting anger control you." Don't let the sun go down while you are still angry, for anger gives a foothold to the devil.

If you are a thief, quit stealing. Instead, use your hands for good hard work, and then give generously to others in need. Don't use foul or abusive language. Let everything you say be good and helpful, so that your words will be an encouragement to those who hear them.

And do not bring sorrow to God's Holy Spirit by the way you live. Remember, he has identified you as his own, guaranteeing that you will be saved on the day of redemption.

Get rid of all bitterness, rage, anger, harsh words, and slander, as well as all types of evil behavior. Instead, be kind to each other, tenderhearted, forgiving one another, just as God through Christ has forgiven you. (Ephesians 4)

A Personal Blessing

In the name of Jesus, Father, I pray for all who have read this book, that they may become complete in you. I pray that they accept Jesus as their Savior and Lord, and with the help of the Holy Spirit, may they fulfill the destiny You preordained for them before time began.

Amen.

www.ingramcontent.com/pod-product-compliance
Lightning Source LLC
Chambersburg PA
CBHW071241090426
42736CB00014B/3175
9780988612907